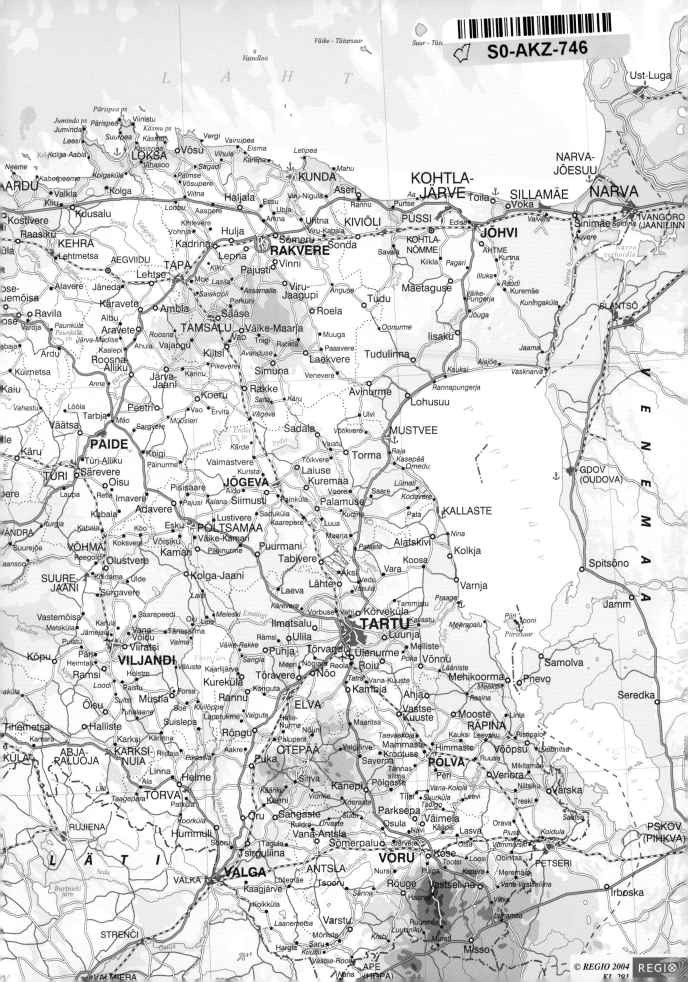

ESTONIA

land
people
culture

Estonia. People, land, culture.

Text by Kristina Porgasaar
Translation- Luisa Translating Bureau
Photos by Toomas Tuul, Ain Avik, Meelis Lokk, Malev Toom,
        Toomas Volmer, Kaido Haagen,
        Lembit Michelson, Arne Ader, S. Stepashko, Aimur Kruuse
Paintings and drawings are from the collections of the Art Museum of Estonia
Design by Jaana Kukk
Language editor- Kadri Liimal
Editor in chief- Aimur Kruuse

© GRENADER GRUPP   www.grenader.ee   372 53 477777

ISBN 978-9949-411-40-5 (paperback)
ISBN 978-9949-411-41-2 (hardcover)

ESTONIA

COAT OF ARMS OF ESTONIA

ESTONIAN NATIONAL BIRD – chimney swallow

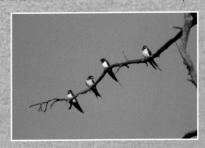

ESTONIAN NATIONAL FLOWER – cornflower

ESTONIAN NATIONAL STONE – limestone

Area:	45,227 km2
State border:	3,794 km
Land border:	633 km
Population:	1,311,870 (01.01.2014, Board of Statistics)
	female 54%, male 46%
Ethnic composition:	Estonian 69%, Russian 25%, others 6%
Capital:	Tallinn (431,021)
Largest towns:	Tartu (97,117)
	Narva (58,663)
	Pärnu (41,528)
	Kohtla-Järve (37,201)
Political system:	Parliamentary republic
Head of State:	President
National holiday:	24th February (Independence Day)
State language:	Estonian
Religion:	Protestant ca 12%
	Orthodox ca 10%
	Catholic ca 0,4%
	Other ca 1%
Highest hill:	Suur Munamägi (318 m)
Largest lake:	Lake Peipsi
Deepest lake:	Lake Rõuge Suurjärv (37.5 m)
Longest river:	Võhandu River (156 km)
Average air temperature:	July +16°C/February –9°C

history

People have lived on the territory of present-day Estonia for at least ten thousand years, which makes Estonians one of the oldest nations in the world. Estonians have managed to maintain and modernise their language. And probably due to their slow and calm nature they have never tried to conquer foreign lands or increase the territory. Once they reached the Baltic Sea thousands of years ago, they decided that the flat land covered in forests was the best for them.

After the peaceful existence of several millennia, they embarked on an unequal fight against crusaders in the early 13th century. By that time, a unitary country had not yet been formed and the only resistance Germans encountered came from separate counties. In 1219, the Danes, led by King Valdemar II, also engaged in the fight. Estonians were unable to endure on two fronts for a long time, especially since the enemies had more contemporary military equipment and better fighting techniques, not to mention the support of the powerful Catholic Church. When in 1238 the land was divided between different foreign powers, following the Stenby Peace Treaty, Estonians lost the right for their own land for centuries. Northern Estonia went to the Kingdom of

Denmark and the rest was divided between the Teutonic Order and bishoprics.

The land was mostly feudalised to vassals who were predominantly of German origin and who would develop their domestic economy by way of manors; Estonians had to start making payments to them for using their own land. This inequality brought Estonians to the rebellion known as St. George's Night Uprising on 23rd April 1343. Some years later, the King of Denmark Valdemar IV sold his possessions to the Teutonic Order.

When Russian Czar Ivan IV declared war against Livonia in 1558, Denmark, Poland and Sweden also got involved. The latter were interested in the political status of local areas and they were afraid the Russian influence would spread to the west. After the Livonian War that lasted for 25 years, the land was once again divided between foreign powers. Northern Estonia went to Sweden, southern Estonia to Poland and the Island

of Saaremaa went to Denmark. The land was ruled by three kingdoms at the same time. Even though Estonia has been subject to more than 30 crowned heads throughout its history, Estonians have never established their own kingdom.

In the first half of the 17th century, Swedish King Gustav II Adolph seized the present-day area of southern Estonia from Poland in the course of a successful military campaign, and in accordance with the Brömsebro Peace Treaty of 1645 the island of Saaremaa, previously under Denmark, went over to Sweden as well. Even though peasants remained dependent on the German manor lord, life under the new rule became considerably easier. The peasantry received the right to submit complaints against the manor lord to the Court Judge, taxes were leveled off and standardised; also, a number of schools were established, where peasants could study reading and religion. The period that is known in history as the Swedish Golden Age lasted only until the end of the century. The Northern War between Russia and Sweden began in 1700 and with the Nystad Peace Treaty of 1721, Estonia was considered part of czarist Russia;

◄ *A symbol of Viljandimaa - Wiiralti or Tammekoori oak*
▼ *Ancient memorials: sacrificial sites and stone coffin barrows*

at the same time, the status privileges of the German nobility were authorised. The situation of the Estonian peasantry worsened – peasants became attached to the land and practically plummeted to the status of serfs. The nobility, however, remained the actual rulers over the land and its people even after the dissolution of serfdom from 1816-1819.

It took an entire century to reach spiritual, economic and political independence. The second half of the 19th century is known as the national awakening, when Estonians were able to muster enough self-esteem to sing themselves into a nation in the First Song Festival in 1869 and to lay a foundation for Estonian culture. The Estonian Independence Manifesto was read out in Tallinn on 24th February 1918, followed by German occupation and war with Russia. Independence had to be fought for in the War of Independence and on 2nd February 1920, by signing a peace treaty in Tartu, Russia was the first to acknowledge the independence of the young country de jure. Independence, however, only lasted for a couple of decades.

In accordance with a secret additional protocol of the Molotov-Ribbentrop Pact concluded in 1939, the Soviet Union forced a military base agreement on Estonia, and a year later occupied Estonia. In 1941, over 10,000 people were deported to Siberia. The occupants changed in the tumult of the Second World War and so the country was under German rule from 1941-1944. After the war, the Soviet regime was restored and the terror continued. Over twenty thousand people from Estonia were deported to Siberia during the night of 25th March 1949. Land and property were nationalised

and life went on according to the instructions received from Moscow. The existence behind the Iron Curtain lasted until 1991.

The election of Mikhail Gorbachev as the Secretary General of the Communist Party in 1985 can be considered the beginning of the new awakening. With his upsurge to power, a new political period started in the Soviet Union, one that was characterised by key words such as 'reform' and 'openness.' At first, this

did not bring about any changes in Estonia. In 1988, a movement that supported perestroika was established – the People's Front. Civil society organisations, associations and movements started to re-emerge. On 16th November 1988, the Supreme Council of the Estonian Soviet Socialist Republic adopted the declaration about the sovereignty of the Estonian SSR. In January 1989, the Supreme Council of ESSR passed the Language Act by which the Estonian language received state language status. On 24th February 1989, for the first time during the Soviet occupation, the Estonian Day of Independence was officially celebrated and the blue, black and white national flag was hoisted up on a tower on the Toompea castle. The long awaited independence,

▲ *Ruins of the medieval Laiuse Castle*
◄ *Ancient stronghold sites: Soontagana and Varbola*
▼ *Open-air events in summer bring joy by recreating the Middle Ages*

however, arrived only a couple of years later – on 20th August 1991. This time, it was the Republic of Iceland that was the first one to acknowledge the independence of Estonia de jure, just a couple of days later, and on this occasion, the former Lenin Square in Tallinn was renamed Icelandic Square.

▲ *Viljandi Castle Hill – picturesque ruins of the castle*
▼ *Kalvi Manor*
► *Kalevipoeg – monument to the War of Independence in Tartu*
► *Pilistvere Cairn; in memory of the deported*

history

people

The Estonian language is the main carrier of Estonian culture; there are over one million speakers of Estonian in the world. The Estonian language belongs to the Baltic-Finnish language group of the Finno-Ugric language family with Finnish as its closest relative. The Estonian language is the official language of the Republic of Estonia, in which books and magazines are published, television and radio programs are broadcast and it is also the language of tuition in general education schools and universities.

Despite a single written language, the Estonian language has retained various dialects. The dialect spoken by the islanders of Saaremaa is understood by the majority of Estonians, whereas the southern Estonian dialect differs substantially from what is spoken in the other regions of Estonia. There are a lot of borrowed words in the Estonian language – borrowing a word from another language has often been considered a better option than inventing a new one. Words are adapted to a more usable form, and with the existence of 14 cases, the absence of grammatical gender and a future tense, they have often changed beyond recognition. A number of Estonians adopted family names that sounded foreign in the 19th century when family names were taken into use. Later, those and also Russian-sounding names were simply

translated into Estonian.

Throughout thousands of years, Estonians have blended with the different nationalities that have settled here. The first immigrants were the Baltic tribes arriving from the south and the Finno-Ugric tribes arriving from the east. The oldest discovered settlement is in the Pulli village near Pärnu and it is approximately 10 000 years old.

The first Germans arrived in Estonia during the crusades. German merchants began shaping the development of city life and the land was ruled by German lords who, being a separate Baltic German class, retained their native language and culture and ruled the land as a higher class for about 700 years until the beginning of the 20th century. During World War II, they resettled in German territories.

In the 13th century, there were coastal Swedes both on Estonian islands and on the western coast. They were law-abiding and had already been baptised two centuries before the Estonians. A lot of them assimilated with the local people and Estonians took over their folk songs and traditions. While during the first Republic of Estonia, the islands of Vormsi, Ruhnu, and Osmussaar, as well as the islands of Pakri and Noarootsi peninsula were mostly populated with Estonian Swedes; after World War II, all that was left was Swedish-sounding place names, as most of them had evacuated Estonia to Sweden in 1944 and those who had remained were deported to Russia by the Soviet authorities.

Village life in Rocca al Mare Open Air Museum

Old Believers who left Russia on religious grounds arrived in Estonian territories in the 17th century and are still living in small communities on the banks of Lake Peipus. They have managed to maintain their culture, religion, Old Slavic church language as well as archaic first names.

During the Soviet times, there was an influx of immigration from the republics of the Soviet Union. Throughout a period of approximately five decades, up to seven million migrant workers came to Estonia, but only a small percentage of them remained here. Most of them regard Russian as their native language, although their ethnic composition is more varied. Accession to the European Union has increased their interest in Estonian language and culture.

▲ *Cemetery on Vormsi Island*
◄ *Katariina Church in Muhu*
► *Villages of Old Believers near Lake Peipus: view from Varnja, prayer house in Raja Village, selling onions*

Estonia is mainly plains and occupies second place in the world with regard to swamps. In southern Estonia the landscape becomes hilly and the view gets wider. This is where the hills of Estonia are located, the highest of which is Suur Munamägi (Great Egg Hill, 318 m). Southern Estonia was freed from glaciers after the last ice age about 14 000 years ago. The Estonian land surface rises in northwestern Estonia up to 3 mm a year – here extra land for the islands is gained each century. All in all, Estonia has over 1,500 islands, but only a few of them are populated.

When comparing the old maps with those of today, we see bays instead of the present-day coastal lakes. With the rising of land, the northern Estonian limestone cliff has partially remained apart from the sea, but there are also various places where the grey limestone walls rise up straight from the sea. The highest of them is the steep Ontika limestone cliff, reaching up to 56 meters above sea level. Valaste waterfall there is, indeed, the highest, but it has been artificially made and the 7-meter-high natural Jägala waterfall is considered the highest. Southern Estonia is characterised by the 400-million-year-old reddish sandstone denudations of the Devonian period, descending as 20-meter-high walls into the river.

Estonia is a part of the Eastern European plain and there are thousands of rivers and lakes here. Lake Peipus is the fourth largest in Europe. Local rivers on

the other hand are short and do not have much water; in fact, some rivers in the karst region in northern Estonia flow partially underground. Despite the large number of rivers, not all the water can be carried to the sea. Moreover, the annual precipitation (550-800 mm) substantially surpasses evaporation, and as a result, the nature is excessively humid and swampy.

Human activity covers a third of Estonia, a fifth of the territory is under swamps and a half is covered by forest. The main types of trees are pine, spruce and birch.

Estonian forests also have aspen, oak, ash, elm, alder and maple. Due to the geographic location of Estonia, many western European plants are here on the eastern border of their natural habitat and several Siberian species on the western border of theirs. Meadows covered with scattered trees are the richest in species, where biolo-

◄ Jägala waterfall in Northern Estonia
▲ Frequently seen wild animals, moose and fox, and a rarity – an osprey

gists have been able to discover up to 74 different plant species per square meter, i.e. 5% of the entire Estonian flora. Over 200 plants have been taken under protection, including 24 orchids that have their natural habitat here.

The more than 60 species of mammals living in Estonia include, among others, the bear, lynx, wolf, fox, roe, elk, wild boar and the beaver. Here one may meet over 300 bird species, including different eagles and the black stork. A tenth of the territory is under environmental protection, including the nature conservation areas of Matsalu and Vilsandi on the western coast, which are bird nesting areas of European importance. Lake Peipus is the richest in fish and is the natural habitat of the Peipsi sparling and Peipsi lavaret, named after the lake.

The Estonian territory is not large, but weather on the coast and inland may differ considerably. The maritime climate makes winters mild and humid (humidity ca 80%) on the islands. The cold and hot temperature records of Estonia have been measured on the mainland, however. The lowest winter temperature was measured on 17th January 1940, when the temperature in Jõgeva fell to −43.5°C. The highest temperature measured in Estonia of +35.6°C was measured in Võru on 11th August 1992. In summer, daylight lasts for about 19 hours but in winter only for 6 hours. Long winter nights become brighter by snow cover that lasts for about three months. Temperatures may fall below freezing even during nights in June and then again in August and the overall growth period lasts only for about 6 months.

▲ *Brent geese in autumn*
► *Panga cliff in Saaremaa – 20-metre-high limestone wall*
► *Moor landscape in Alam-Pedja Nature Reserve*

tallinn

Tallinn was first placed on the world map by Arabian geographer al-Idrisi in 1154. The city gained fame in the 14th-16th centuries as a member of the Hanseatic League. From behind the Iron Curtain, Tallinn achieved international recognition as the host of the yachting regatta during the 1980 Moscow Olympic Games and then again as the capital of an independent state when the medieval old town, which is preserved in a rather complete form, was entered into the UNESCO World Heritage List in 1997.

Throughout the times, the city has had many different names. For instance, the Russian chronicles refer to a stronghold called Kolõvan that was situated here. After it was conquered by the Danes in 1219 and a fortress was built here, it was called *Taani linnus* (the Danish stronghold) by Estonians. With the passing of the centuries, the name has been shortened to Tallinn. The Scandinavians called the cape reaching out to the sea Lindanäs. Germans and Russians, however, called it after the county nearby respectively as Reval and Revel.

Every year, a small grey-haired man comes out of Ülemiste Lake to see whether Tallinn is ready. The correct response to the old man of Ülemiste is that the city is far from being ready and that there are several houses under construction and that it would definitely take years before all the work is completed. If someone answered that the city was ready, he would open the floodgate on the very same day and let the water run down from Lasnamäe to the valley and drown the entire city.

The geographically favorable location of Tallinn has always brought recognition to the city. Tallinn was on the trade route from the Varangians to the Greeks during the time of the Vikings, and from Western Europe to Russia in the Hanseatic time. Even today, the port of Tallinn is one of the largest ports in the Baltic Sea. Through Tallinn, transit trade is conducted with Russia and Tallinn is one of the places visited by cruise ships en route to St. Petersburg. Within the last decade, the traffic on the

Tallinn-Helsinki line has become one of the densest in the world; during the Soviet time, passenger transportation here was rather infrequent.

Tallinn has always been the capital of Estonia – the center of economy, trade and culture. Even though Tallinn has expanded throughout the centuries, partially also at the expense of neighbouring areas, the Old Town has still remained the hub of city life. The actual development of the city and its division into the Upper Town or Toompea (Dome Hill) and the Lower Town

▲ *Aerial view of the seaside town*
▼ *Medieval Hanseatic town: St. Olav's Church on the left, St. Nicholas' Church on the right*

that functioned as a city-state began with the arrival of German merchants in 1230. In 1248, the Lübeck town bylaws were adopted and by the end of the century, Tallinn was a member of the Hanseatic League. The economic heyday of the city was in the 14th and 15th centuries, and most of the buildings in the Lower Town date back to that period. Life is still centered around the Town Hall Square. One of the oldest enterprises in Europe is here, the Town Hall Pharmacy (1422), which is still functioning in its original spot. In addition to the Pharmacy and Town Hall (1404), other Gothic buildings in the Lower Town have also been preserved to this day thanks to the law from the 14th century to build buildings of stone. Later, a number of buildings have received a newer and fancier appearance both from outside and inside during the reconstruction. Houses of the nobility in Toompea, on the other hand, have been built up again after the fire of 1684.

There are ten different churches in the Old Town today. Most of them date back to the Middle Ages, when in addition to convent churches each district had its own church. One of the oldest churches is the Dome Church that was consecrated in 1240. St. Olav's Church, dedicated to the Norwegian saint, was built in the area of the former Scandinavian market place and was with its 159 meters the highest building in the world during the Middle Ages. St. Nicholas' fortress-church, built in another town district, was dedicated to St. Nicholas, the patron saint of seamen and merchants.

Money was not an issue when it came to defending the city in the 14th -16th centuries. Medieval Tallinn had over 60 towers and the city wall was almost 4 kilometers long, about 3 meters thick and 16 meters high. By today, only Toompea Castle and 1.85 kilometers of the town

wall with towers around the Lower Town have been preserved.

The development of the city received a new boost in 1870 with the opening of the Tallinn-St. Petersburg railway. The biggest development, however, took place during the Soviet time, when the area of the city increased noticeably and the population soared from the pre-war couple of hundred thousand to over half a million. By now, the population has decreased considerably. The building of monotonous concrete high-rise areas, such as Mustamäe, Õismäe and Lasnamäe, did not so much solve the lodging problems of the local people as it increased immigration from the so-called sister republics of the Soviet Union.

Present-day Tallinners see the city as revolutionary, developing and active, powerful and fast, a center of money and power. Even though the inhabitants are city-centered, they love variety and their favorite places are the Old Town, Kadriorg Park, Pirita beach and the so-called City area.

◄ *Medieval defence buildings: Danish Fortress and the city wall with towers*
▲ *Downtown: Short Leg and a medieval merchant's house*
◄ *Medieval festivities – the Old Town Days*

◄ *View of the city centre: Town Hall Square, Town Hall, Town Hall Pharmacy*
▼ *Views of the Bay of Tallinn: silhouette of the city centre, Pirita Convent, Olympic Sailing Centre*

tartu

Tartu is a university town, the town of the Emajõgi River, a city of sculptures and the capital of Classicist architecture. Tartu is also the cradle of Estonian culture where the major events of the national awakening took place in the 19th century. Various national societies were established here, such as the Learned Estonian Society, Vanemuine Society, Estonian Farmers Society, as well as the Estonian Students Society, whose blue-black-and-white flag that was consecrated in 1884 later became the national flag of Estonia. The First Song Festival was held here in 1869. Also, the peace treaty between the Republic of Estonia and the Soviet Russia was signed in Tartu on 2nd February 1920.

Nearness to a navigable waterway fostering trade and the elevation offering protection against enemies lured people to Tartu in ancient times. With the further development of the region, the swampy area near the Emajõgi River was also exploited. The stronghold is first mentioned in old Russian chronicles when the armies of Kiev prince Jaroslav the Wise conquered it in 1030 and established a fortress called Jurjev here. Not long afterwards, the fortress was retaken by Estonians, but a couple of centuries later it went to Germans and received a new German-sounding name, Dorpat. The town became the center of the bishopric, city life developed and by the end of the 13th century, the town was a member of the Hanseatic League.

Once upon a time, two students in love were strolling around the city of eternal youth and love. When they were standing in front of the Town Hall, it suddenly started to rain from the clear sky. The young man opened his umbrella to protect the girl from the rain. The enticing closeness of the beloved and the warmth of summer joined the two in a kiss and the girl wished – let it be like this forever. At that very moment, thunder clapped and lightning struck, and the two young people were turned into stone. And this is how they are standing even today, defying the rain and joined in an eternal kiss under the umbrella.

The new heyday of the town arrived after the Altmark Truce was signed in 1629, after which the larger part of Livonia went under the Kingdom of Sweden and Tartu became the administrative center of the guberniya ruled by a governor general. The first university *Academia Gustaviana* was opened in 1632 during the rule of the Swedish King Gustav II Adolph and Tartu became a university town. The university was closed during the Northern War. A century later, when the university was re-opened in 1802, Tartu gained in prominence – this time as a center of science and research of the Great Russian Empire.

The town received its architecturally homogeneous

appearance during the restoration after the fire of 25th June 1775. The requirement for the Classicist façade types laid down for the buildings in Russia was followed, as in addition to the harmonisation of laws, administration, etc., common requirements for architecture were also being worked out. Tartu became the capital of Classicism – the Athens of the Emajõgi – and local buildings became models for designing both city palaces and manor houses. In addition to dwellings, the university also required new buildings in the early

◄ Dome Hill: monument to K. E. von Baer, Ruins of the Dome Church
▲ Gustav II Adolf, King of Sweden and the founder of the University of Tartu
► Kissing students in front of the Town Hall
▼ Main building of the University of Tartu

19th century and this is when the Anatomical Theater, University Main Building, clinics and the Observatory, which was technologically advanced at the time, were built according to the designs by J. W. Krause. The Botanical Gardens and library were opened as well.

The interests of the Baltic German elite and of imperial Russia guaranteed the sustainability of Estonian educational life. The only Baltic scientist ever to have received the Nobel Prize, the founder of physical chemistry, Wilhelm Ostwald (1853-1932), was related to the university. Also, Karl Ernst von Baer (1792-1876), the founder of modern embryology and Yuri Lotman (1922-1993), the founder of the Tartu school of semiotics, have worked in the university.

Even though men of Estonian origin had been admitted at the university as early as the middle of the 19th century, the University of Tartu was not opened as a national university with Estonian as the language of tuition until 1st December 1919. In 1921, female students made up a quarter of all students and in 1945 over 50% of the students were female. Today there are over 15,000 students and the university receives foreign students from a number of different countries. Despite the fact that foreigners were unable to visit Tartu during

youthful and their fellow citizens are perceived as carriers of the mentality of the town. Tartu does not leave anyone indifferent. Anyone who has visited Tartu and got to know the spirit of the city will dream of returning here again.

the Soviet time, the city managed to maintain its international reputation.

By now, Tartu has once again become a classical university town and both the city and the university are open to foreign visitors. In addition to education, the economic and political life has also been given a boost during the last decade. The inhabitants of Tartu describe their town as mild, sensitive, warm, friendly, and

▲ *Town Hall Square: Town Hall and a Slanted House*
◄ *Small House of the Vanemuine Theatre, Angel's Bridge, fair in the Town Hall Square*
▼ *View of the city centre and the modern skyscraper, dubbed 'the Flask'*

pärnu

Pärnu is the summer capital of Estonia, a city of parks and of the beach where Estonian summer life converges. Pärnu is in the heart of Estonians and the local area has been inhabited for over ten thousand years. The first newspaper in the Estonian language, the Pärnu Postimees, has been published since 1857. Many people loved by Estonians are related to Pärnu, the poetess Lydia Koidula (1843-1886), musician Raimond Valgre (1913-1949), and the chess player Paul Keres (1916-1975). Moreover, the Estonian Independence Manifesto was first read out in Pärnu in the evening of 23rd February 1918.

Pärnu is situated in the river delta and probably due to the good location two towns were established here in the 13th century. The port on the right bank of the river was already mentioned in 1241, but after the looting raids of Lithuanians the importance of the stronghold on the left bank increased. The present-day downtown has developed from the so-called New Pärnu that had emerged near the stronghold of the Order and was first mentioned in 1265. The small and wealthy settlement of merchants and artisans received town bylaws rather soon and became a member of the Hanseatic League by the end of the century.

The new heyday of the town arrived in the 19th century when the development of the town into a holiday resort began. The first bathhouse was completed

in 1838, and heated seawater baths were offered as treatment. Later also the healing impact of sea mud was proved. The development of the holiday resort was greatly furthered by picturesque sandy beaches with a low southward bay and by Beach Park as well as the lanes set up in the town. The building of Mud Baths, completed in 1927 on the site of the original bathing establishment, has become a symbol of the resort town.

The imposing Art Nouveau Ammende Villa was completed in 1905. Lively construction activity in the city continued only after a couple of decades, when the development of Pärnu into the number-one holiday resort of the Republic of Estonia began. In addition to self-awareness, the wealth of Estonians had grown and the villas built in Pärnu had to represent a new architectural style, one that differed from all others. Since the late 1930s, Pärnu could be considered the Estonian capital of Functionalism. *Rannahotell* (Beach Hotel, 1937, designed by O. Siinmaa, A. Soans), representing the crème de la crème of Functionalism along with *Rannakohvik* (Beach Café, 1939, designed

---

◄ *Ammende Villa*
▲ *Assembly Hall and Beach Park*
▼ *Mud Baths*

by O. Siinmaa) whose mushroom-shaped balcony is still the heart of the summer capital were both completed. Rannakohvik is the place where a number of concerts, parties, beach volleyball competitions and other events are organised.

Pärnu was a well-known resort town during the Soviet time. But Estonians were only able to enjoy beach life or a holiday in the summer cottage, as the limited number of treatment vouchers were allocated through the trade union and all over the former Soviet Union. For visitors without a voucher, local housewives offered bed and breakfasts, which was one of a few forms of private business at the time and could only exist under the pretense of fostering friendship between nations. By now, the former health resorts have entered a new era and the majority of SPA visitors are Finns and Swedes.

▲ *Pärnu Old Town*
▶ *Beach Hotel and new concert hall*
▶ *Bustling beach in the summer capital by the mushroom-shaped balcony of the Beach Café*

There are about 50 towns in Estonia, the oldest of which is Tartu that received its town bylaws in 1230. Tallinn, Pärnu, Haapsalu, Viljandi and Paide received town bylaws in the 13th century as well. The largest city is the capital Tallinn with its 400,000 inhabitants and the smallest are Mõisaküla in southern Estonia and Kallaste in eastern Estonia with about a thousand inhabitants each. Over half of the population prefers to live in towns. In the 15th century, there were 8 cities in the territory of present-day Estonia, several of which were members of the Hanseatic League. The construction of the railway in the second half of the 19th century fostered the emergence of new towns. During the Soviet occupation, the cities grew thanks to large industrial plants that were established here.

In addition to the official capital, Estonia also has Pärnu as the summer capital, Türi as the spring capital, Otepää as the winter capital and Põltsamaa as the autumn wine capital. Põltsamaa also used to be the capital of the Livonian vassal kingdom from 1570-1578. Some Estonian towns have remained on the other side of the border after the lands were divided, for instance Valga had to be divided between neighbors. Now the larger part of the town belongs to Estonia and the smaller part to Latvia.

At exactly midnight on a full-moon August night, the White Lady who once lived in the castle in an enigmatic way appears in the church window of Haapsalu Castle. Namely one of the canons had once, violating convent rules, brought in a woman, who was disguised as a choirboy. But after a while, the trick was revealed and a search revealed that the choirboy was in fact a woman in men's attire. The canon was sentenced to death through starvation and his mistress was walled alive inside a church wall, from where she sometimes appears on full-moon summer nights.

The charm of the small towns lies in low wooden houses with high gabled roofs sunk in lavish green gardens, old churches and castle ruins. Pärnu, Kuressaare, Narva-Jõesuu and Haapsalu are known as peaceful summer resorts. They are characterised by sandy beaches with shallow warm water, beach promenades, and assembly halls with a brass band playing on the bandstand. In the early 20th century, these were the favorite places of holidaymakers from Sweden and Russia. There is a *singing bench* in honor of the famous Russian composer Pyotr Tchaikovsky who used to spend his summers in Haapsalu. The bench is located on the spot where he would often come to marvel at the sunrise.

Alternatively, the life of a small town can also only

be related to industry, as in towns of northern Estonia – Maardu, Kohtla-Järve and Sillamäe – or to the military, as in Paldiski, which was established in 1718 by Russian Czar Peter the Great as a marine fortress and a military port. Paldiski went to the Soviet Union under the Military Bases Agreement in 1939; in 1968, a nuclear submarine training center was established here, and the area was closed and surrounded with barbed wire. For the next couple of decades, Estonian authorities had no idea what was going on in the town. The last Russian troops left Paldiski as late as in 1994. Currently

---

◄　*Haapsalu: Assembly Hall by the sea and the singing bench*
▲　*Centre of Valga*
▼　*Ruins of the Haapsalu Castle*

the town is connected to military affairs and the Peace Operations Center of the Estonian Defense Forces is located here.

▲ *Ox – the symbol of Rakvere (Tarvanpää – Ox's Head – in the Middle Ages) and the Lutheran Church*
▼ *Ruins of the Rakvere Castle*
► *Viljandi: suspension bridge to stronghold hill, ruins of the castle, town center*

Virumaa has the greatest contrasts in Estonia: the most picturesque scenery and the dreariest artificial landscapes. This is also where the highest limestone bank in Estonia is situated (in Ontika) commanding a most magnificent view of the sea, the most impressive park in Toila, the forests and swamps in Alutaguse untouched by human activity, high gangue and ash hills, but also the greatest number of different nations.

Baltic Finnish tribes – the Votians, Izhorians, Vepsians, Ingrians and Karelians – used to live on both sides of the Narva River. The coastal people were actively involved in trade even as late as in the early 20th century and communication between the people of Virumaa and the Finns was so intense that Estonia is still referred to as Viro in the Finnish language.

For 800 years, the Narva River has divided the two civilisations – Orthodox and Catholic. Nowadays the river also unites the two worlds, so that the Hermann castle built by the Danes on the Estonian side in the 13th century and the Ivangorod fortress built on the Russian side in the 15th century form a military-architectural pair. The great number of fortified buildings on the road from Narva to Tallinn is also indicative of the age-old danger accompanying proximity to the border. In addition to the Narva Hermann Fortress, there are the Toolse and Rakvere

The Virumaa region also has several places that are connected with the ancient Estonian hero and hero of the national epic, Kalevipoeg. His final resting place is claimed to be in the depths of local forests. It is rumored that before another enemy attack, he and his company hid a great treasure they had gathered over a long period of time in a nearby hill. There were expensive beads, silver coins, old crosses and items of gold among them. The treasure received from victories is sought to this day, but so far no one has found it.

strongholds and the fortified dwelling house established in Purtse in 1533, but also Vao and Kiiu tower fortresses and Jõhvi, Lüganuse and Haljala fortress churches.

Even though Narva received town bylaws as early as in 1345, its greatest heyday came only in the late 17th century, when the Swedish king started to restore the town after the fire. Narva was supposed to become a model Swedish town, the second capital of the kingdom and the administrative center of Ingermanland. However, the heyday was cut short. Two battles of major importance were fought near Narva in the Northern War (1700-1721). In the first one, the Swedish King Charles XII was victorious over the Russian army that was several times bigger, but the second battle was won by the Russian Czar Peter the Great. After the war, Narva and all of Estonia went under the rule of Czarist Russia.

The town was not left intact in World War II either. The greatest concentration of firepower on the Eastern Front was located near Narva and the almost desolate town was bombed to nothing on 6th March 1944. Today, only the Town Hall and the fortress remain of old Narva. After the war, new life started in the town with new people.

The foundation for the local industry was laid in 1857, when one of Europe's greatest enterprises of the time, the cotton mill by the name of Kreenholm manufactury, was established. The world's most powerful waterwheel of the time was built on Narva Waterfall. In addition to using cheap hydroelectric power and advanced technology, this was the first time when the new philosophical-architectural concept of an industrial campus was carried out. In addition to the production facilities also administrative and public buildings, as well as the church and residential buildings were built in the same complex. The manufacturing was successful and the local textile production was awarded Grand Prix in the world exhibition in Paris in 1900.

Virumaa is the most important industrial region in Estonia thanks to oil shale. The first mine was opened in Kukruse in 1916, but decades earlier, the owners of Kukruse manor, the von Tolls, had used the burning stone in the furnaces of their distillery. Later, the stone received its scientific name, kukersite, after the site of discovery. Today, it is mainly used in producing electricity and in the chemical industry, although initially it

---

◄ *Historical buildings in Narva: Hermann Fortress and the Town Hall*

▲ *Ruins of the Toolse Fortress and Purtse fortress-residence*

was also used for making oil shale gasoline. Oil shale provides the majority of Estonian electric energy and the two local thermal power stations cover over half of the needs of the country.

During the Soviet time, several heavy industry enterprises were founded in the area, as a result of which the population increased by several times. For instance, on the place of the former Sillamae resort, a military industrial town was built in the 1950s. The town was intentionally not marked in the maps of the Soviet Union, and Moscow or Leningrad was first used as the address of the citizens of Sillamäe. German prisoners of war and soldiers of the Soviet army were involved in the construction works. As money was not spared, the town of Sillamäe is still an exemplary model of the architecture and city planning of the Stalinist era. The main employer in the closed town was the military plant of strategic importance. The plant used local natural resources to produce uranium oxide; when resources were depleted after some years, uranium ore was imported from elsewhere.

The establishment of a phosphorite plant was planned in the middle of the 1980s, but the foundation of phosphorite mines would have meant a natural catastrophe for Estonia and an even greater influx of foreign labour. In a new political situation that had just

an icon of the Falling Asleep of the Virgin Mary found here as well as by a spring with healing powers down in the valley.

emerged, people dared, for the first time to oppose the authorities and the anti-phosphorite campaign supported the freedom movement, which eventually brought about the restoration of Estonian independence.

One of the most beautiful active convents is situated in Virumaa. Pühtitsa Orthodox Convent commenced its activities in Kuremäe in 1892 and was supposed to contribute to the spread of orthodox religion in the predominantly protestant country. It was founded in a place that was regarded as a sacred hill by both Lutheran and Orthodox believers. Namely, the Virgin Mary had appeared to local peasants here in the 16th century and the right choice of place was further confirmed by

▲ *Artificial landscapes: Baltic Thermal Power Station, ash hills and emerald lakes*
◄ *View of the Gulf of Finland*
▼ *Kuremäe Convent*

Southern Estonia has the highest hill, the deepest lake and the longest river in Estonia. Also, the thickest oak, known by the name of Tamme-Lauri (8 meters in diameter, 20 meters in height, and 680 years old), depicted on the Estonian 10-kroon note, grows here. Võru was the hometown of Friedrich Reinhold Kreutzwald (1803-82), the writer of the Estonian national epic Kalevipoeg, sculptor August Weizenberg (1837-1921), a pioneer of national art, Jakob Hurt (1839-1907), a great figure in Estonian cultural history and it is said that the Russian Empress Catharine I grew up in the neighborhood.

There are several nature preservation areas in southeastern Estonia for the protection of local terrains, bogs, swamps, caves, rivers, primeval valleys and even bats and ants. One of the most unique ones is the Akste ant colony with over a hundred anthills on an area of 200 hectares. The biggest anthill is about 5 meters in diameter and the highest is over 2 meters. The number of

In the old times, the land was almost as flat as a board. The Devil could not stand it, because when the land is flat, it is difficult to lead people to do dark deeds. So he went to God and said: "Let's make the world a little smaller, it is too big." God agreed and they rolled up their sleeves. The Devil went to the north and started to push the land from there. God went to the south and started to slightly push the land. He had figured out the Devil's plan. This is how Võrumaa and Tartumaa got their hills. And she who does not believe it can go and see for herself that there are more hills in Tartumaa than there are in Võrumaa.

"inhabitants" reaches over 3 billion.

The local landscape was shaped by the Ice Age, which deepened the valleys and piled up hills. There are several primeval valleys in the region, the most beautiful of which is considered to be the Rõuge primeval valley (10 km in length, up to 75 m in depth). The Rõuge River flows through several consecutive

lakes, the largest of which is Rõuge Suurjärv. The lake with its depth of 38 meters is the deepest in Estonia. Of other valleys, the largest is Ööbikuorg (Nightingale Valley), which was named after nightingales' singing on spring nights and the most unique is Hinni Canyon with a reddish Devonian sandstone denudation of about 400 million years.

The most famous of the denudations is Suur-Taevaskoda ("heaven's chamber"), with its good acoustics. It rises as a 20-meter-high palisade straight from the river. The caves and 150-year-old primeval forest have been the source of several legends. The Piusa River primeval valley has the highest sandstone denudation in Estonia – the Härma Mäemine wall (43 meters). The Piusa caves were formed as a result of manual mining of sand from 1922-1966 and are situated nearby. The goal of the local nature preservation area is to protect the habitat of thousands of bats wintering in the caves.

Võrumaa is known as the hilliest region in Estonia, and has many scenic views. The highest hill is Suur Munamägi (318 m). Beautiful hilly landscape lures people to engage in outdoor activities both in summer and in winter. The land here is covered with snow for

several months and the area is popular as a winter sports center among top Estonian skiers, several of whom live near Otepää. The first Tartu Marathon was held here in 1960 and since 1995, skiing marathons have been held in the Worldloppet series. The longest distance is 65 km from Otepää to Elva, but depending on weather conditions, the track has also been shortened.

Rich archeological findings indicate that Finno-Ugric tribes used to live here about 10 000 years ago, but now the Setomaa region is divided between Estonia

---

◄ *View from Munamägi and the Emajõgi delta*
▲ *Munamägi viewing tower*
▼ *Kallaste sandstone outcrops*

and Russia. The small Seto tribe has managed to retain its unique language, culture and customs. Once a year, they elect their own king. Local people celebrate traditional holidays of the folk calendar as well as all holidays of the Orthodox Church. The lead singer of the women's choir at festivities knows at least ten thousand verses by heart. National costumes are worn during festivities. Female attire with red variegated embroidery accompanied with kilos of silver jewelry is particularly fancy.

The Suur-Emajõgi River flowing through Tartu heads to Lake Peipus, although the ancient river in the same place was flowing in the opposite direction at the end of the Ice Age. Even now the river changes its mind a couple of kilometers after Lake Võrtsjärv, turns around and flows backwards. Once also the Pärnu River was called the Emajõgi and until the 18th century, the rivers served as an important waterway from Pärnu to Pskov. The lowland near Lake Peipus is known as a swamp by the name of Emajõe Suursoo and came into being thousands of years ago when the northern bank rose and caused the flood of the southern bank. By now the swamp landscape covers over 20,000 ha. Bog islands and reed beds have lured here not only eagles but also other rare bird species.

There are around 12,000 swamps in Estonia covering about a fifth of the territory. The formation of Meenikunno bog started about 8,000 years ago and different bog development stages can be seen here. A swamp is a self-regulating system and the peat there serves as a filter for polluted precipitation and contaminated ground water. The bog water is very clean but slightly acidic and that is why swamp biota is poor in species. It is said that the Swedes built a boarded track through Mennikunno bog during the Northern War. Today, there are boarded tracks built for visitors almost everywhere in Estonia and bogs can be easily crossed.

In winter, it is possible to get anywhere across the ice and this is when both fishermen and skiers can be seen on the bodies of water. The famous Battle on the Ice was fought on ice in the southern part of Lake Peipus on 5th April 1242 where the Russian troops lead by the Prince of Novgorod Alexander Nevsky defeated the Teutonic Order and stopped the advance of Germans toward Russia. Since then the lakes have divided the Orthodox world from the Catholic. Alexander Nevsky was canonised in 1547 and even in Estonia there are

several Orthodox churches dedicated to him.

◄ *Piusa caves and sandstone outcrops on the Võhandu River*
▲ *Seto female choir*
▼ *Moor in Teringi Landscape Reserve*

◄ Lake Võrtsjärv and Karula National Park in winter
▲ Picturesque winter in Southern Estonia
▼ Tartu Marathon

Once
upon a time there lived
a hero named Töll on the island of
Saaremaa and his relative, Leiger, on the island of
Hiiumaa. The giants had to fight their enemies and the
Devil, but once in a while they would also test their strength
with each another. But in general they got along fine and once they
even planned to build a bridge between the two islands, though the
water was not even knee-deep for the giants. The bridge building was
not carried out at the time, because they thought being separate was
better, but some stones that were carried to the place can still be seen in
the sea. Their wives were also tall and strong. But once when they
were carrying stones for the sauna stove, their apron ribbons
broke and the stones fell down. Piret's stone can be seen in
Laimjala on Saaremaa Island and Tiiu's stones
in Soela Strait on the coast of Hiiumaa.

The largest Estonian island – Saaremaa – is for Estonians the dreamland of summer-time holiday-making, for the Scandinavians it is the land of ancient gods and to the world it is the home of Fabian G. von Bellingshausen (1778-1852), the discoverer of the Antarctic. One of the smallest inhabited islands, Kihnu, is the home of the legendary Estonian captain Kihnu Jõnn.

Owing to the fact that the Vikings have stayed on the islands, the islands have belonged to the king of Denmark as well as to the Teutonic Order and that coastal Swedes have lived here, the islands have got foreign sounding names in addition to their Estonian names. Hence the largest islands in Estonia: Saaremaa, Hiiumaa, Muhu and Vormsi are also known as Ösel, Dagö, Moon and Ormsö. Most of the islands are situated in the Baltic Sea. All in all there are over 1,500 islands in Estonia and just a tenth of them are inhabited.

Even though traces of human activity date back to as long as 8,000 years on several islands, some of the islands are but a couple of thousand years old and they provide an opportunity to view the formation of soils and greenery. The flora and fauna on the islands is extremely rich owing to the maritime climate, limy soils and varying landscapes and there are dozens of rare species growing here, including virtually all kinds of orchids found in Estonia. Local coastal areas are the habitats of seals and across the islands goes the route of migrant birds between Europe and the Arctic; several of the islets serve as gathering and nesting places of birds and are of European importance.

The greatest number of meteorite craters discovered per square kilometer in the world is in Estonia. For instance, the traces of a crater caused by a meteorite that fell millions of years ago can be seen near Kärdla in Hiiumaa. The Neugrund meteorite crater, the biggest in Estonia, is situated near Osmussaare. One of the most recent, the Kaali meteorite, fell during the time when the area around the Baltic Sea was already inhabited. The tales about the coming of the Sun to earth and of the burning of Saaremaa are not only found in the local tradition but also in the folk stories of neighboring countries and the perishing of the son of the Sun in Greek mythology is likely to be a reference to the same event. The diameter of the largest crater, known as Kaali Lake, is 110 m and its depth is 16 m.

The mystical formation of Kaali Lake can also be seen in the unusual ceiling paintings of Karja Church depicting a magic protection circle made of various pagan signs. The signs refer to a joint fight of earthly and heavenly forces against evil, they offer protection against a demon of fortune appearing in the form of a fiery flying dragon and the tripod is the symbol of both eternity and the Sun and its broken leg is likely to refer to the local solar catastrophe. Karja Church was completed in the 14th century and, according to a legend, it has been named after Saint Catharine, the daughter of the Sun. The church was a resting place for pilgrims on their way from Scandinavia to Livonia across Gotland.

Lighthouses on the islands have shown the way to seafarers for hundreds of years. One of the oldest lighthouses in Europe – Kõpu lighthouse – has become a symbol of Hiiumaa. In addition to lighthouses, not more than a century ago, almost every village had its own windmill, but by now only a group of five windmills has remained on a windmill hill in Angla village, Saaremaa. The post windmill has become one of the most beloved symbols of Saaremaa in addition to junipers and home-brewed beer. The Emu windmill on the island of Muhu is the only working windmill in the region. Almost every village on the islands is known for thatched roofs, lath and stone fences. The best known is the village of Koguva on the island of Muhu that has been integrally preserved and gives a good overview of a typical village where houses are sited haphazardly. About a hundred buildings have been preserved, the oldest of which dates back to the 18th century. The old thatch-roofed barn houses are still the hearts of the farms, housing both the living quarters and household facilities. Old boats are resting upon moss-covered stone fences.

There are few towns on the islands. Kuressaare, the capital of Saaremaa, is the largest and the oldest. The town emerged near the bishopric stronghold built in the 13th century and received town bylaws in 1563. As the stronghold has not suffered considerable damage in wars, it is the only integrally maintained medieval fortification in Estonia. It has been owned by the Germans, Danes, Swedes, Russians and Estonians. The moat-enclosed convent building received its present-day appearance in the 14th century. The eagle symbolising St. John, the patron saint of the stronghold, gave the name Arensburg to the town, which was later translated into Estonian. Kuressaare is a holiday destination with summer and health resorts. Strolling on the beach and in the town center in the Classicist style seems refreshing. Only in Kuressaare can one still find a well-preserved town hall in the early Baroque style (1670), a weigh house (1664) and a triangular town hall square.

During the Soviet time, islands were in the closed border zone region with a visa regime. To visit an island one had to have a good reason or a letter of invitation from relatives. Several islands were closed to visitors and

▲ *Lake Kaali*
▼ *Details of Karja Church*

their former inhabitants had been relocated before the establishment of Soviet military bases.

The inhabitants of the small island of Kihnu have managed to retain their old folk traditions and rural way of life owing to the isolation of the island. Only in Kihnu can one see women wear hand-woven skirts of the national costume every day. In fact, the wealth of a woman is determined by how many skirts she has, and the number may reach up to twenty. Younger women wear a bright red skirt or one with less red, an older woman's skirt has less red, a skirt with blue stripes is worn as a sign of mourning for at least a year after the loss of a close person. The skirt follows fashion and while only some years ago shorter skirts were in, now long skirts are back with narrower stripes. The tradition of springtime wooing is still alive on the island, celebrated with eating, drinking and dancing and when the groom finds a belt in his pocket, the wedding can be held the next summer. The

◄ *View of Saaremaa: windmill, junipers, horses*
◄ *Stormy Bay of Paabu at Ristna on Hiiumaa Island*
▲ *Piret and the Giant Tõlll*
▼ *Stone fence in Koguva Village*

unique Kihnu culture space was entered into
the UNESCO list of oral and intangible world
heritage in 2003.

- ► *Kõpu lighthouse in Hiiumaa*
- ▼ *Steep cliff*
- ► *Kuressaare Castle in Saaremaa*

lahemaa

Lahemaa National Park – the largest and the best known is situated in northern Estonia. The Park was established on 1st June 1971. The area of the national park is 72,500 ha. Lahemaa provides a good overview about the nature and history of Estonia as well as about village development and manor houses.

The region was uncovered from the glacier sheet about 11,000 years ago, and the first people arrived here about 8,000 years ago. Traces of receding ice can be seen in beach ridges, sand dunes, boulders, deep lakes as well as the swamps that have emerged as a result of lakes or rivers growing over. Thousands of boulders have remained in local forests and beaches after the ice melted, the most interesting of them are Majakivi ("a house stone") with a 30-meter-diameter and Jaani-Tooma Suurkivi ("the Great Stone of John and Thomas"). The earliest traces of human activity can be seen in round barrows of stone that are approximately 2,500 years old. A lot of them are found in Muuksi.

Huge piles of stones that were piled up during famine can still be seen in the fields of Palmse estate. Palmse masters took good care of their peasants and once during a severe crop failure they also helped the people of the neighborhood. He who had strength to come to Palmse was given grain from the granaries which were so blessed they never ran empty. The masters did not ask for any work or help, but people, and there were hundreds of them, decided to clean up the stones from the fields and this is how these huge piles of stones came into being.

Lahemaa is away from larger centers and the most important roads, and the human settlement was in the past and still is relatively sparse. This has helped preserve unique natural landscapes, which was one of the reasons for establishing a national park here. Today, around 70% of the territory is composed of natural landscapes, most of which are forests of different types. Also, alvars with their thin layer of soil, thousands of junipers and

rare plant species that have evolved over a couple of thousand years in cooperation between the man and nature are also of interest. Almost all animals living in Estonia have been spotted here: brown bear, fox, wolf, lynx, beaver, etc.

It is believed that the region might have been relatively unified and was called Revala up to 13th century. The oldest known place of settlement is Kahala. In the 13th century, the Cistercian monastery received plots of land in the neighborhood from the king of Denmark as a token of gratitude for the services provided in baptising. And this is how Tallinn St. Michael's convent established an estate in Palmse and Roma Cistercian monastery from Gotland founded one in Kolga. By the 15th century, there were a dozen manor houses in the area and most of them belonged to the Baltic German nobility. By today, impressive manor houses have been preserved only in Kolga, Palmse, Sagadi and Vihula. Palmse is the most complete of them all. Today there is a visitor center of Lahemaa National Park in Palmse. The Sagadi estate is used by the Forest Museum and Kolga was returned to its former owners, the Stenbock family, from Sweden.

Palmse estate was obtained in 1677 by the von der Pahlens, who lived there until 1925. Local lords held high positions and Carl Magnus von der Pahlen brought luxurious high society customs to his estate while being in the service of the Russian czar. His son Alexander nearly bankrupted the family, when he undertook to establish the Tallinn-St. Petersburg railway.

The present Palmse manor house dates back to the late 17th century, and it was rebuilt in 1785 during the heyday of the Baltic German culture. The two-story manor house was the center of estate life. The festive hall was on the first floor and the bedrooms were on the second floor. The house was traditionally divided into the lord's and lady's sides. The kitchen and servants' rooms were located in the basement. Nearby were the stable-coach house and granary. The distillery and steer stable were further away. There were around twenty buildings altogether, the most luxurious of which was the greenhouse, which was high fashion in the 19th century and allowed grapes, roses and palm trees to be grown. Producing spirits and growing steer were the main sources of income. They would travel to Tallinn for the season with a large staff of servants, and would stay there from Christmas to Easter.

Each manor had several villages; Palmse was one of the largest. It enjoyed not only better natural conditions but also bigger farmsteads and more people. Even though Estonian peasants were serfs and lacked the freedom of movement, living conditions under this estate were generally better than in some neighboring ones.

Villages in Lahemaa were small. For instance, there were slightly over ten families living in Altja in the late 19th century. The seaside village has retained its appearance to this day. Farm buildings already back then had glass windows and chimneys, although characteristically living quarters and husbandry facilities were under the same roof. And through the window one had to be able to see the barn doors, because that is where the main property of the people was stored: food and clothes. For fire safety reasons, saunas were built away from other buildings. By now, there is only one inn in Altja instead of the former three. Next to the inn was the hill with a swing where people would come together on Saturday nights, swing, sing and dance as well as talk about village matters.

Views of Lahemaa

In coastal villages fishing played an important role in addition to agriculture, and there were a lot of people on the cape who went out to sea in the mornings. Each group of boatmen had their own shed for nets at the end of the cape. The main fish species caught were Baltic herring, salmon and houting that would later be smoked using alder wood. In addition to fishing, the boats were used for transporting firewood and construction stones to Tallinn. For centuries, the so-called 'sweetheart trading' across the sea between Estonians and Finns served as a cover for the smuggling of salt and spirits. Looting the ships that had landed in stormy weather was a commonplace activity and the men of Altja can be called 'skilled' coastal pirates. But almost all people of the neighborhood should have been taken into custody for robbing some larger ships.

One of the biggest Estonian ports of the 19th century was in Käsmu. In 1884 a Maritime School was established here. When it started to teach master mariners, the village turned into a wealthy captains' village, where almost every family had its captain and there were altogether 62 of them. As their wealth grew, the captains would build modern dwellings with glass porches. The heyday of Käsmu ended in 1944, when the Soviet authorities confiscated the ships, burned the boats and closed the coast with barbed wire and a ploughed strip of coastline. Those who could, escaped to the west, and many of those who stayed were deported to the east. The free sea has called the coastal people back and the village with its white houses against the background of the blue sea is one of the most beautiful villages in Estonia.

▲ *Altja net sheds at the tip of the cape*
► *Palmse Estate: park and the manor house with a view of the interior*

The first public art exhibition was held in Tallinn in 1798, but it was not until the mid-19th century that the first Estonian artists went to study at the St. Petersburg Academy of Arts. Even though the local artistic scene was quite lively at the beginning of the century, the Baltic Germans were still the main creators and consumers of art until the beginning of the 20th century. The best-known art collections were in the Raadi estate of the von Lipharts and in the Vääna estate of the von Stackelbergs. Even though the families took the lion's share of their collections along with them to Germany, some paintings came into the collections of the Art Museum of Estonia.

The heyday of Baltic German culture in the 19th century also had a positive impact on the development of art. The overall cultural exchange with Germany became closer – artists and writers came to Estonia and people went from here to Germany to study. Articles were published about those who went to study and teach at the Düsseldorf Academy of Arts. Baltic German artists drew their themes and inspiration from depicting the Estonian peasants. Both Carl Timoleon von Neff (1804-77) and Oscar Hoffmann (1851-1912) have idealised peasant women wearing

national costumes and peasant men sitting in an inn, which was characteristic of the time.

The first professional Estonian artists were painter Johann Köler (1826-99) and sculptors August Weizenberg (1837-1921) and Amandus Adamson (1855-1929). Owing to their diligence and talent, they quickly reached a high artistic level and Köler's painting "Truu valvur" (Faithful Guardian) and Weizenberg's sculpture Hamlet were displayed in the world exposition in Paris in 1878. Amandus Adamson's Russalka (1902) was the first monument in Tallinn that was designed by an Estonian artist. Estonian society started to consume art only in 1920, when a bronze copy of Weizenberg's Linda was set up in Toompea (Dome Hill) in Tallinn.

The next generation of artists also studied in St. Petersburg and Germany, visited not only Paris but Italy

◄ *Johann Köler. Faithful Guardian. Detail. 1879*
◄ *Oskar G. A. Hoffmann. Peasants Playing Cards. 1880*
► *Karl Timoleon von Neff. Estonian Peasant Woman with a Child. 1859*
▼ *Johann Köler. Girl at a Spring. 1859-61*

as well and drew inspiration from travels to Finland, the Crimea, Greece and North Africa. In the early 20th century, people wanted to study art in their homeland and they started to look for the national element in art. The life of Estonian peasants and folk tales were depicted in the works of art of Estonian artists. Ants Laikmaa (1866-1943) and Kristjan Raud (1865-1943) are the pioneers of Estonian national art. In addition to their creative activity, they also organised Estonian cultural life and held studio-schools in the beginning of the 20th century.

The first professional art education establishment of Estonians, Pallas, was opened in Tartu in 1919. The later renowned graphic artist, Eduart Wiiralt (1898-1954), was one of the first students of the school. Having already studied in Paris earlier, he went back there during World

War II. Even though several artists emigrated at the end of the war, many decided to stay at home. Among others who stayed was also Adamson-Eric (1902-68), who tried to advance the Estonian art scene on the spot. Being one of the founders of professional Estonian applied art, he became the director of the Tallinn State Institute of Applied Art. As a number of other executives, he was also subjected to Stalinist repressions and had to resign in 1949.

From world art, the masterpieces of two Lübeck masters from the end of the 15th century are exhibited in St. Nicholas' Church: Herman Rode's main altar (1478-81) and the beginning of Bernt Notke's Dance Macabre. The valuable masterpieces of world art from later periods are displayed in the Kadriorg Art Museum in Kadriorg Palace. Also, the Palace can be regarded as a superb piece of art. The construction of the palace began in 1718 under Russian Czar Peter the Great and his architect, Niccolò Michetti. The main hall in the Baroque style, reaching through two floors, is a real piece of art and it has virtually retained its original appearance. The museum displays art from the Netherlands, Germany, Italy, Russia, Austria, Switzerland and other countries. Also, the new building of the Art Museum of Estonia will be in Kadriorg Park.

Estonian national culture has been influenced by western and eastern traditions, and throughout the centuries, both Christian and pagan worldviews have melted together here. Although the country is small, regional differences can be rather substantial. Nowadays genuine national culture is seen less and less, although the cultural environment in the Seto region and on the island of Kihnu have succeeded in maintaining their integrity despite changes.

Earlier, farm families used to adhere strictly to all folk holidays and traditions. The traditions of rural people have found their way into towns as well, and for example on Shrove Tuesday people slide down hills everywhere. Bean or pea soup with pettitoes and Shrove Tuesday buns are eaten. Bones are used for making spinners for children. In November, young people enjoy going from door to door wearing masks, singing songs and wishing good luck with crop and cattle to kind families on the eve of St. Martin's Day and St. Catherine's Day. In return, they expect to receive good treats.

On St. John's Eve, bonfires are lit all over Estonia with people singing and dancing around them. Jumping over the fire and baking jacket potatoes in the ash have become a tradition. With holidays, usually forecasting future and superstition are connected. For instance, during the short St. John's night, one has to find a flower from a fern and girls who are of marriage age

have to be able to pick 7 flowers from 7 gardens having climbed over 7 fences. They then make a bouquet of these flowers, tuck it under the pillow and they will dream of their future husband. St. John's Eve also marked the end of springtime entertainment – swinging – and the beginning of summer work. Almost all young people of marrying age fit onto the swing. Usually the swing was built by the young men of the village and they were the ones who did the swinging; girls would bring them presents and sing. The bolder would even take the swing over the shaft and swing all the way over. Today, swinging has evolved into a competition sport – *kiiking* – where the length of swings allowing the swinger to go over the top bar is measured.

meat is smoked there.

◄ *Midsummer night with a bonfire and swinging*
▲ *Smoke sauna*
▼ *Village youth on a swing*

During Christmas and at New Year's Eve, people eat a lot. Even now the tradition is followed that there have to be 7 dishes on the table at that time, including the Estonian national dishes of baked potatoes with pork and sauerkraut and blood sausage with cowberry jam. Also fish, gingerbread, apples and hazel nuts have to be on the table. It was believed that if a man ate 7 dishes, he would have the strength of 7 men in the following year. At night, bread is taken to animals in the stables and the food is left on the table until the next morning, because it is believed that the souls of ancestors come home to eat at night. The food had to be prepared by the lady of the house, and the beer was brewed by the master. The custom of brewing homemade beer and offering it to neighbors and visitors is still alive. The homemade beer of Saaremaa Island is claimed to be so strong that the second jug would land a mainland lad under the table. In addition to beer, light ale is still a popular soft drink.

The sauna is still a vital part of the life of an ordinary Estonian. The sauna has never been a luxury, but a necessity and people usually used the sauna on a Saturday night. In addition to washing, whisking in the sauna was considered to have spiritually cleansing powers. The sauna is part of the St. John's Night festivities, birthday and anniversary celebrations as well as company parties, and the verbal contracts concluded in the sauna would not be reneged later. The sauna was also the place where people came into this life as well as departed from here. The sauna may also serve the purpose of a summer kitchen and a laundry room and

song festival

Every five years, singers and dancers from all over Estonia gather in Tallinn to participate in the Song and Dance Festival. The festival starts with the joint parade of the participants from Vabaduse Square to the Song Festival Grounds, followed by a concert given by a choir of up to 20,000 singers to approximately 100,000 spectators. Up to 8,000 dancers dressed in national costumes perform a dance show in a sports stadium. The festival usually takes place in the first weekend of July, but participants practice their performance together throughout the entire previous week.

The first Song Festival was held in 1869 in Tartu as the Anniversary and Thanksgiving Festival for the 50th Anniversary of the Abolishment of Serfdom. The initiators of the festival were Johann Voldemar Jannsen and the first Estonian society – Vanemuine – that was established on his initiative in 1865. Festival participants included men's choirs and brass bands, all in all 845 people. As Estonian national music had not been studied much by that time, songs by German composers were used. Also, two songs were performed in the Estonian language. The lyrics of both of them were written by J.V. Jannsen's daughter, Lydia Koidula. A song *Mu Isamaa, Mu Õnn ja Rõõm* (My Fatherland, My Happiness and Joy) by the Finnish composer of German origin Fredrik Pacius, was performed, and the lyrics were written by Mr. Jannsen himself. The song became popular with people and was officially made the Estonian anthem in 1920. The authorities then did not perceive the Song Festival as a political statement, but for the Estonians the festival had deep cultural and political implications for future self-determination. The third Song Festival was already held in Tallinn and the pretext given to Russian authorities for the festival was the 25th anniversary in honor of Russian Czar Alexander II and the fourth Song Festival was held in honor of the 10th anniversary of Russian Czar Alexander III.

During the Soviet occupation, the desire to hold song festivals was great and more and more people wanted to participate in them, and so the new and bigger Song

Festival Grounds were completed in 1960. But the reasons for organising the festival had to be sought in red holidays and, in addition to Estonian songs, other songs had to be performed. Several songs, including the Estonian anthem, were banned altogether. The song written by Gustav Ernesaks, a well-known conductor and the proponent of the song festival tradition, *Mu Isamaa On Minu Arm* (My Fatherland is My Love), was then sung as an unofficial anthem.

As with the first song festival the Estonians turned themselves into a European nation, the demonstrations of 1988 based on the tradition of song festivals saw the nation sing itself free. At the beginning of the anti-Soviet demonstration period in 1988, tens of thousands of people gathered in the Tallinn Song Festival Grounds during the light June nights to sing patriotic songs. The first public claim for the restoration of Estonia's independence was made in the mass event called The Song of Estonia on 11th September 1988 with approximately 400,000 people present. This groundbreaking period in Estonian history later became known as the Singing Revolution. Now, just as more than a century ago, the yearning for freedom and the need for self-realisation of the nation was so great that it joined people together in the pursuit of a single goal. No more permits or pretexts were sought for holding a public festivity; instead, it was through singing and the desire that was whispered together – we will become free anyway – that the Republic of Estonia was restored on 20th August 1991.

The activities of Estonians have also encouraged neighbors and song festivals have become a tradition in Latvia and Lithuania, as well. In 2003, the song and dance festival tradition in the Baltic States was listed in the UNESCO list of oral and intangible world heritage. To mark Estonia's accession to the EU on 1st May 2004, tree planting bees were arranged during the first week of May, where the participants of this year's Song and Dance Festival and volunteers planted a million new trees in Estonian forests. Estonia brings its song and dance festivals and green thinking to Europe.

Song Festival in Tallinn Song Festival Grounds